THE GENTLEMAN'S GUIDE TO THE NASTY DIVORCE

BY E.B.GUNN

Published by GunShy Press
email to: gsp@gentlemansguidetodivorce.com

Copyright © GunShy Press, 2012
All rights reserved

www.gentlemansguidetodivorce.com

cover by: Maker
www.makerny.com

ISBN-10: 0985489243 (pod softcover)
ISBN-13: 978-0-9854892-4-3 (pod softcover)
First Edition

Grateful thanks to my editor, A.B.,
who believed in this book and worked hard on its composition.
And over-the-top thanks to my best pal, S.S.,
who contributed to this book in innumerable ways.

TABLE OF CONTENTS

PREFACE

I am not a lawyer. I am a club man with many dear friends. Some
are rich. Some are handsome. Some are famous. Some are drunks.
Some are womanizers. And some are family men. Some I've
known 50 years. Some I met more recently. Most by now have, like
myself, divorced at least once.

It is my own divorces, and those of my friends that inform this book.
Where what is written here appears to be advice, it is not *legal*
advice. Only lawyers legitimately give legal advice.

I can suggest to you where to drive the boat, and why you might
want to go there. If you want to know how to get the boat started,
ask your lawyer.

E.B.Gunn

THE GUIDE TO THE GUIDE

Divorces have a rhythm. This book is organized chronologically in accordance with that rhythm to give the reader a heads-up on what might be next along the way. It isn't pretty sometimes, but please permit me to assure you that you'd rather know what's coming than be blindsided by it.

Part 1: The first five chapters address life when one spouse, but not the other, is setting a course towards divorce. (This period can be disarmingly hopeful.)
The remaining chapters in Part 1 describe highly charged situations that can occur in the days after both spouses see they are headed for a divorce. (This part is ugly.) Part 1 is concluded at a milepost, the Temporary Hearing, where the rough draft of the terms of a divorce get drawn.

Part 2: These chapters describe the period between the Temporary Hearing and the Final Hearing, which in real life can be 9 months to 3 years, or occasionally even more. (This part can be the ugliest – but you'll get through it.)

Part 3: You're past the crisis, but not quite out into the sunshine. Part 3 describes situations and solutions on divorce-related topics in the days and years after a divorce is finalized.

If you're facing divorce, but there are no children or custody issues* involved:
you might want to skip the chapters that describe custody fight issues. These chapters are: Cohabitation, The Cops, Kids 1, Affidavits, Kids 2, Eerie Echoes, The Club, The Track, Wild Cards, Kids 3 and Holidays.

From time to time legal terms are used.
The first time these words or phrases are used they appear in **bold**. While they are defined when they are introduced, these terms also appear in the glossary at the end of the book.

*If you're even thinking about a custody fight over a dog – or any pets, read the custody chapters. There's help for you, but it's expensive.

FORWARD

Love, you wouldn't lie to me…would you?
-Boz Skaggs-

How in the world did YOU get here? It's the big D…the thing you never really thought would happen to you (or maybe you *did* see it coming even as you stood at the altar). Whatever string of events may have brought you to this crummy moment, life is lousy today and it's hard to see the way out. If that's how you're feeling, then this book is for you.

Cheer up, it's actually going to be alright.

This isn't a psychology book to hold your hand and make you feel better. This is a survival manual. I'm just a pal from the old school who has learned the hard way and who, when I was in the depths, wished there had been a book like this for me to read. Instead I had to pay my attorney (billable hours, youch!) to teach me what so many before me had learned, and might have shared with me.

Hard as it is to believe, there are countless good guys going through the exact thing you are right now – and many more have preceded you. Later, they'll talk about their divorces, and many of their stories will sound similar. However, when the cheese is hitting the fan, we don't call our divorced pals to ask them what to expect next. We access this information by paying many thousands (that could have gone into a new Patek Philippe, Beretta, Donzi, Maserati!) to a lawyer, because, I guess we think, "*Mine* is the worst one ever." I certainly felt that way.

So let's just say you're sitting at the bar over a scotch with a divorced buddy. If you've got kids in the mix, chances are your buddy will say the cards are stacked against you and solidly in the favor of the mother. Maybe so, but don't panic. Once you know a little about the playbook (yes! In essence, there *is* a divorce playbook), you and your attorney can salvage a lot more than you think: time with the kids, money, and a good bit more that might be important to you. But your buddy has a point: women's liberation seems to reign royal in the Family Court system. Mommies and daddies aren't equals in that courtroom. Whether he killed the marriage or was the one who held it together, right or wrong, it is the Dad who will be expected to give lots of money to the ex who is supposed to spend it on the kids (and not on Botox, as of course she may).

Just to get a fair shake, guys should know the basics on how to proceed – some of the tried and true tricks nearly every divorce attorney will use (yep, what's possibly in store for you). That's what this book's about. If you know a little bit going in, and you can control your temper -- better still, bring some humor to the case, you'll maintain your dignity and at the same time, maybe not get, well, pardon my French, screwed.

But first, let's start at the beginning, with the thing that got you to here. Let's start with love.

Sir Isaac Newton said for every action there is an equal and corresponding reaction. More homers come off fastballs. Every public relations executive has repeated the axiom: "the higher you fly, the further you fall".

And so it is with love and marriage. If you had a laconic marriage, chances are you'll probably have a laconic divorce. Conversely, if you had a passionate, make-love-on-the-Haitian-sands, stay-up-all-night-crying-and-screaming, tear-up-the-old-girlfriends'-pictures-and-throw-them-in-the-fire sort of marriage, then chances are you're going to have a corker of a divorce. Sir, this book is for you. (P.S. if this "passion" appeals, then you may have this divorce thing happen to you more than once, or twice ... but hey!)

So, for starters let's consider it important and comforting to remember Sir Isaac Newton right through every crisis in the process. Let Sir Isaac provide you with your new orientation. Every time the ex does something over-the-top nutty, your reaction should be to recall utterly silently to yourself a time that was over-the-top great. Because now you're paying for that time. Sometimes the best things in life aren't free. You just pay later.

Chin up. Greater, and perhaps even crazier things, if that's what you're into, await you on the other side of this nasty stretch. You'll get there just fine - with a little help from your friends, and the hard-won wisdom in this little book.

Read on.

THE BRAZILIAN

Part of being a gentleman is being honest, especially with yourself. Overwhelmingly most marriages end because of someone else -- the *other* man or woman. Okay, so now it's time to face reality. You wouldn't be looking at this book unless you had an inkling - or more - about where your life/marriage is headed.

The "we've grown apart" stuff is a convenient myth left over from boarding school. If you're hearing "we've grown apart" or words to that effect as a recurring theme around the house, what it means is your wife thinks she's got the other guy pretty well hidden.

HERE ARE JUST A FEW CLUES YOUR WIFE MAY BE HAVING AN AFFAIR:

- ➤ She gets a Brazilian bikini wax. (And doesn't want your attention.)
- ➤ She mysteriously starts losing weight – and isn't griping about the diet.
- ➤ Over your objections she wants new boobs.
- ➤ She gets a new "look".
- ➤ She's asking for the house or other assets to be put into her name or, if they are in your name solely, into joint ownership.
- ➤ She's saying she needs an account of her own (of your money) to feel better about herself.
- ➤ She buys a bunch of fancy and skimpy underwear.
- ➤ She's all-of-a-sudden concerned about child-raising issues that never concerned her in the slightest before.

One very smart and streetwise pal of mine believed the "grown apart" stuff right up to the day after his divorce was finalized when he learned his wife was pregnant. And, may I add with discretion, not by him.

HERE'S HOW YOU FIND OUT FOR SURE:

> ➢ Study her cell phone call records, especially the after-hours calls.
> ➢ Scroll through her emails.
> ➢ Check out the diary you find in her underwear drawer.
> ➢ Casually ask her best friend (listen to the music, not the words...watch her eyes closely. By the way, if your wife's best friend is a heterosexual *he*, then you're an idiot.)
> ➢ Hire a private investigator.

Or, OMG, it's not her ... it's you!

PLAYER

Okay, believe me I get it. There was this cute divorcee who was so full of life, yet so misunderstood, that you chose to take a moment to see if you could help her. And that moment turned into several hours during which you found yourself, as a way of comforting her, of course, confessing that the things that were wrong with her marriage are also wrong with yours. The cute divorcee, it turned out, was not the only one who was misunderstood. Oh no! Nor was she the only one seeking comfort. Roger that! As if by magic one thing led to another. And, well, it is magic. Isn't it?

So now you own it, or at least you're making payments on it. What was easy at first is becoming more complicated, but no way will you give it up.

Things at home have changed too. Intuitively your wife knows what's going on, but she's in denial – or maybe not. No matter what, things just aren't the same...

HERE ARE THE CLUES YOU'RE HAVING A MARRIAGE-ENDING AFFAIR:

> ➤ You're gone a lot more. (*Another* evening meeting?)
> ➤ There's odd stuff (dinners, jewelry, trips, huh?) on the credit card bills.
> ➤ Your wife's not getting the nookie she used to get.
> ➤ You're irritable with her.

Now you're in the club of guys who've beaten the odds before, and who are feeling lucky. Some will and many will not, and the success of those who do and don't will rest substantially on the sagacity of their wives. So ask yourself, how easy is it to deceive her? And how good are you at deception? Were you able to fool your teachers in school? Your parents? Have you successfully juggled simultaneous girlfriends in the past? And what's the likelihood the cute divorcee will permit this part-time arrangement to go on indefinitely? Can her silence be purchased? Is the price affordable?

If you're in this situation, you'd better get honest with yourself. Chances are, you'll get caught. If you know you're not going to be able to ditch the girl because you love her too much, then figure out a way to get a **separation agreement** ASAP. Getting out in front of your divorce will save you bundles down the line – more on exactly why later.

Sure, you say, getting separated is smart, but it's too messy. The present arrangement, having it both ways, is easier. You've got the home life when it suits you, and the cute divorcee gives you the love that dried up at home. Why make trouble when there isn't any?

But much more likely is that you're just not sure. Will the new thing last? Is it worth betting the farm on?

Now it's time to give your wife the benefit of the doubt – she may be in denial now, but intuition almost always wins out.

HERE'S HOW SHE'LL FIND OUT FOR SURE:

- ➢ She'll rifle your phone, emails, and credit card bills.
- ➢ She'll ask your secretary – or your best friend's wife.
- ➢ She'll hire a private detective.

Ah, yes. The private detective. He'll be your best friend, or your worst enemy.

Private Investigators

In about half the states in the U.S., as of this writing, there is a "fault" provision in the divorce code. Fault means, in effect, one or the other spouse did something to cause the divorce. If it can be proven, the court may assign that individual responsibility for causing the dissolution of the marriage.

The grounds for divorce are typically these:
> ➤ Adultery
> ➤ Desertion
> ➤ Separation
> ➤ Mental cruelty
> ➤ Physical cruelty
> ➤ Drunkenness or drug abuse

A private investigator can help you with proving any of these, although separation's pretty obvious, but their stock in trade is adultery, and as adultery is by far the most common culprit with the summer house crowd, it is the focus here as well.

Often there are consequences before the law for being "at fault," especially for wives. These could be, depending on the circumstances and the state law, less or no alimony (which saves you a bundle), less visitation for her (which can mean less child support from you), and less custody for her (which for you can mean a greater voice in the children's affairs, which may also save you money). These considerations are why private detectives stay in business. It is also true that plenty of tramps have been shown in Family Court to be good mothers, and so they have gotten the kids *and* generous child support too. SO IF YOU LIVE IN A "FAULT" STATE AND SHE'S CHEATING, AND YOU WANT OUT, CATCH HER. Then, at least before the Judge, you'll be playing on a level field. A good PI can save you a lot of money.

So let's say you've got an inkling she's up to no good. She wants to visit her parents in another state more often. She has a friend in trouble and needs to be with "her" a lot. Even though business has slowed, her office has assigned her more travel than ever. She has decided that she really does enjoy a 2½ hr. workout in the mornings after all. She's going through a "tough time." She just needs some time away to think things through.

Depending upon the individual circumstances there are hundreds of products and gadgets that are designed to put at ease the minds of jealous spouses. There is a link in the "Survival Gear" section of this book's website, www.gentlemansguidetodivorce.com , to a firm that sells them all.

If you conclude there's another guy in the picture, control yourself. DON'T CONFRONT HER. She'll just go to ground, which is to say if she knows you're chasing her, she'll be a lot tougher to catch.

You may know what you know, but now you need to prove what's happening or else you're faced with attorney trick #1: unless you have REAL proof, you're the jerk. They sell you to the judge as controlling, mean, jealous (*"see, he's trying to say I was having an affair when I would never do such a thing."*) overbearing, cruel -- whatever, and she just can't stand to be married to you any more. Unless you have real proof, the kind that will stand up in court, you've got nothing but trouble. So before you confront her or go meet with attorneys, do what you'd never thought you'd do -- the few dollars you spend here may well save you many dollars later: hire a private investigator. If on the basis of your own amateur research you can give the PI specific instructions, that is all the better. He'll spend less time on the case, and he'll cost you less money.

DO NOT TRY TO DO YOURSELF WHAT A PI DOES.

Unexpected things happen out there in the bushes when passions are high. A couple of years ago, the talk of the town was about a married guy who was canoodling at home with another man's wife, while his own wife was at the beach house. When our man heard noises outside, he assumed the rustling around in the bushes was a PI sent by his girlfriend's husband, and peppered him with birdshot. Who was the trespasser? Yep. A power company lineman who had showed up to reset a transformer. So now old deadeye has tipped his hand, the girlfriend was seen (as she ran out the front door with her brassiere in hand), the utility company is suing -- and what do you suppose the theretofore in denial wife at the beach house concluded? Nothing helpful to the fortunes of old Wyatt Earp. If *you* had been your own PI in that situation, old Earp may have taken you out.

Then there was the fellow who took it upon *himself* to spy on *his* canoodling wife. He thought he could rest his case with a photo or two of her misbehaving. Things took an unexpected turn however, when the partiers called the cops on the photographer in the bushes who ended up with a ride downtown and a peeping tom rap. You can bet he's got a story he doesn't want to tell when he gets asked why he's on the Sex Offenders' List – for good.

Hire a pro.

Here's how:
> Determine where you think the adultery is going on, then:
> ➤ Call the heads of security at a couple of the 4 or 5 star hotels in that area and ask them for recommendations.
> ➤ Ask a local domestic law attorney who practices in that area.

!! DO NOT SEND A PI ACROSS STATE LINES.
GET ONE FROM THE AREA WHERE YOU WANT THE WORK DONE.

Laws vary from state to state. What PI's do they don't do alone -- the local guys know the local cops, and the local security officers at the hotels and nightclubs. They know the limo drivers and the back roads. They know the ways things are supposed to be, so they know when something is out-of-the-ordinary.

If you live in a **no-fault divorce** state, don't bother with a PI. Sorry. You're in for a rough ride because in the courtroom it won't matter how many guys she was sneaking around with. Adultery means nothing to the courts in these states and divorces can get pretty crazy. If you don't know whether your state law recognizes fault in divorce cases, type "no fault divorce states" into your favorite browser.

Hiring a PI may cost you a few thousand dollars. That's NOTHING compared to what you would have to spend trying to prove adultery otherwise. Wives (and husbands) having love affairs rarely sleep alone. So if you don't catch her the first or second time, it's probably because she wasn't up to anything. (And maybe you ARE a jealous and controlling nutcase and she's going to leave you anyway unless you get help.)

Private eyes have some pretty sophisticated tools at their disposal. It may be that the fellow will catch your wife cold and she won't even know it. What you want from him is a very specific **affidavit** stating what he knows of the matter, and of course his willingness to testify about what he knows, if necessary, later. All of which is standard stuff in PI World.

A favorite PI device is what they call in the trade "trackers." These are two magnetized GPS platform devices, one of which the PI secretly affixes to the undercarriage of your wife's car and the other of which is surreptitiously affixed to the suspected paramour's vehicle. You announce you have business out of town. The PI sits in his office monitoring the locations of the trackers until the two cars meet. That the two trackers are shown to be together may be all the PI needs. To prove adultery, it is not necessary to photograph the two in bed together. "Inclination and opportunity," when they are shown to exist contemporaneously, are sufficient.

But, just to illustrate the garden variety example, if the trackers show that your wife and her paramour were at the paramour's place from 9:00 P.M. until 5:30 A.M. one evening while you were out of town, and the PI goes over there at 2:00 A.M. and photographs the two cars there together, and he puts what he knows in his affidavit to which he attaches a time-stamped photo of the cars, you've got more than you need.

Okay. So now you know what you need to know…and you don't want to kiss and make up. Instead you see your long-awaited chance to get out on your terms. You've seen the future, and it's not what you signed on for.

Be cool. You have some more work to do.

SLIPPING THE HOOK

Or, let's say it's *you* who is the intended subject of the PI's affidavit. Fair enough. These things do happen...

If you wish not to get caught with your girlfriend, do what the cops do when they're protecting someone, don't fall into a pattern. Don't tell ANYONE where you are, and if the kids ask, give them a phony answer. While you may provide your children with the truth, your children are not "owed" the truth. (Please don't tell me you said yes when your 14-year-old son asked you if you smoked pot when you were a kid!) And you're not helping your best friend by confiding in him. He can be subpoenaed, and probably will be. At the moment of his deposition you have put him in the no-win position of (1) giving up his best friend, or (2) perjuring himself.

For the purposes of hotels, meals, plane fares, rental cars, nightclub charges, jewelry, credit cards and phone bills used in connection with what has become your secret life, create for yourself a separate identity. If you have an attorney, ask him to set up a credit card account for you that gets billed back to his office. He pays it and sticks the charge on your monthly bill. Because of attorney-client privilege these bills are outside the view of your wife and her lawyers. If you want to successfully keep your secret life a secret, do this as soon as you begin your secret life. Second best, and way down the line, is to set up an LLC and put the card in its name, sending the statements to the LLC's post office box for which you hold the only key. If the LLC doesn't have any revenues, you don't have to pay taxes on it.

Pay for her with these cards only.

If your car has OnStar, park it somewhere it belongs and use your girlfriend's, or better still a rental. The OnStar GPS platform component features a system that permits those with the correct password to always determine the exact location of the car. This is handy if your car gets stolen, but it's a major problem if your wife's using it to track you down. Depending on the circumstances, walk, ride a bike, take a scooter, or grab a cab to meet her (limo drivers talk!). Because of the trackers, even if you don't have OnStar, don't trust your car.

If your location can be determined by tracking your mobile phone, leave it in the car. Pay cash or use your lawyer's card to get a Cricket-style pay-cash-as-you-go phone. With these phones there's no bill. When your pre-paid minutes are up, the phone dies. Keep it well hidden, and only talk to her and text with her on it. When that one's used up, throw it in the river.

Good luck – an extraordinary few pull it off. I had a pal (yes, in the 21st Century, and no, he never struck me as a rocket scientist) who had two families (but just one wife). And Family #1 never knew a thing about Family #2 until they met at his funeral.

Chances are, at some point, you'll get caught. If you do, deny it from the start and with vigor. Attack the PI (*are you kidding, you listen to him – that Police Academy flunky?*), his credibility and his "other agenda". Do what you can to suggest you've been set up.

Fudge, deflect, parse, obfuscate and DON'T ADMIT ANYTHING TO ANYBODY until you've talked to your lawyer.

More of the Same

So you got caught. *She* got caught. Maybe nobody got caught – you just want out. Whatever the circumstances, it's curtains. The End. The fat lady is singing. There's no turning this sinking ship around. We're going down. Game Over. Your marriage is ending.

Here are the clues that your marriage is over:

> ➤ You find yourself irritable when you're around your wife.
> ➤ The two of you search for ways to be apart.
> ➤ The dog looks more attractive than she does (I mean, you'd rather go hunting, running, anything with your dog than stay home with the old ball-and-chain – the one you used to call "Sweetheart".)
> ➤ When you're with your wife you're thinking about the girl.
> ➤ You sleep back to back with your wife. Always.
> ➤ You think she smells bad. Even her laugh is annoying. No, nearly everything she does is annoying.

Here's what you'll do to get on with it:

> ➤ Give her the "it's-not-you-its-me" talk.

➢ Force a fight and get to the "it's inevitable" part.
➢ Just leave and call her from London (note: this is the most expensive option).

Often in deteriorating marriages wives say: *"If you divorce me, I'll make sure you'll never see the kids!"* You may have heard this kind of talk emanating from her moments of despair. Some divorced guys don't see much of their kids, but that's usually because they choose it to be that way. If you get divorced and you want to have a hand in raising your kids, the judge is going to give you time with your kids -- even if it was you who was cheating and your wife is a saint (even if you've never been to a parent-teacher conference). The system, while it favors the moms, acknowledges that it is preferable for both a mom and a dad to raise a child, even if they live in different houses. So don't hear it when she threatens you with losing sight of your children.

As the reality of the impending divorce sets in, the threats will come. *"You know they're going to give me the house," "The kids are going to hate you," "I'll make your life a living hell," "By the time you get done paying for the kids and me, you'll be living in a cardboard box down by the train station!"* etc. While it may be sad to hear these things out of the mouth of your former sweetheart, they're not to be feared. The system is designed to mitigate the crises caused by vindictive spouses. Believe me, the courts have seen it all – as have the attorneys. To prevent these bad things from happening is why, in fact, you get a lawyer.

You could have avoided this, you hound -- you could have laid up, gotten the separation agreement and bypassed the expensive alternative. But you had to be Tin Cup and go for the hole.

Or maybe it was you who surprised her with being savvy enough to catch her with the tennis pro. The marriage is over, your wife is in shock – but she's not going to be hang dog for long. No matter who did what, in a startlingly short time, she'll find every reason imaginable to KNOW that you are, in fact, horrible. Gentleman – schmentleman. Enter the attorneys.

LAWYERS

Okay, the 8 bedroom mansion in the Hamptons (along with spare quarters over the stables) just weren't quite enough to make her happy. She needed a little something else. And that little something happened to be Greg the yoga teacher who was camping, you guessed it, in the spare quarters over the stables. And while you were in Florida on business the new security camera you just installed nailed the little lady getting nailed.

So now it's time to get a domestic attorney.

These will be tough times for you. By all means find a lawyer you can get along with. If you can, find one who can make you laugh. Family law is one of the simplest, most common sense areas of the law. You don't need a constitutional scholar to handle your divorce. You need a frat man. Ask around about his/her record: does this lawyer appeal often – if yes, run for your life. That attorney will drag your case out and cost you a fortune. You need someone who's sat across the chess table from other divorce lawyers and knows the game. And you need someone who'll get you out with as much of your own skin as possible.

Sometimes before taking your case and announcing their fees, lawyers will ask you to fill out a bunch of financial disclosure information. DOING THIS IS TANTAMOUNT TO OPENING THE TREASURE CHEST FOR THE PIRATE'S INSPECTION. Get the lawyer's hourly fee BEFORE you disclose your annual income and net worth. Only a chucklehead believes there's no correlation between high salary/net worth and high attorney's hourly fees, and your chucklehead days are behind you, right?

Your lawyer may have to lead you to forensic accountants, attorneys with other specialties, guardians, and perhaps do some judge-shopping (see "Judges") too. It will pay in the long run to get one who knows his or her way around your town or city.

Some domestic attorneys carry the reputations of killers: they'll play to your competitive "we'll chew her up and spit her out" side. Resist vindictiveness – it'll cost you a year's adjusted gross (at least) and still get you the same split you could have achieved for far less.

Here's the reality: chances are you'll keep what you had before the marriage and split up the money (including the value of the jointly-held real estate) you and the ex made and saved during the marriage. If your livelihood permits you to care for them on a daily basis, and you want to, and your lawyer successfully makes that case, the children's time will be divided approximately the same: 50-50. A word of caution: if an attorney says he can get you more than that, beware. There better be a very good reason.

The big reputation domestic lawyer might be worth it, if there's a special wrinkle to your particular situation (like there are going to be lots of reporters wanting to monitor the progress of the case), but if it's pretty plain vanilla, you're wasting your money and probably just prolonging the inevitable 50-50 split. And the longer the whole ordeal goes on, the more you're paying lawyers and the longer you're putting off getting on with the rest of your life.

If you can get to a resolution through **mediation** and a separation agreement, do it. You and your kids will win: the kids won't be dragged through the system, your friends won't get dragged into the courtroom, oh, and you'll save a bundle.

Timeframes vary from state to state, but if you can get a separation agreement and successfully live apart for six months to a year, you're going to be home free. This is the alternative that cuts the lawyers out, and thus it is rarely advanced with vigor by lawyers.

Sadly, mediation doesn't succeed often enough, because the soon-to-be ex is also getting counsel. And if she's been caught with Greg, she's after anything she can get. This is especially true if your wife is approaching 50, that age when some attractive women become desperate thinking they're going over the hill. Greed is at the heart of most nasty divorces. Second place belongs to anger.

But let me not get ahead of myself.

So let's just say you've caught her and she doesn't know yet. Before you go serving her with papers, get with your lawyer and get organized. For example, it is now, while she is unsuspecting, that you and your lawyer want to set the trap that when she falls into it, she will have been shown to the judge at the temporary hearing to have lied. If you can, disable her credibility right out of the starting gate.

There's more. Think about what your wife will do, where she will go when she is in distress, and get there ahead of her. This important defensive concept applies especially to preventing her from getting the lawyer she will want. How do you do this? You know who the top domestic lawyers in your town town are. In big cities it's well known who the society dames use. And if you don't know these things, you can easily find them out. You know who her friends used. You know who's hot. Call them up and go in for an initial consultation. Making it up as you go, tell them a little about the case from your point of view. If you're concerned your wife may find your girlfriend, tell them you have money offshore. Or visa-versa. You do this because lawyers talk around the courthouse, and these lawyers may feel you "had" them a little, which you did. Insist on paying them a few hundred dollars each for their time.

Several things will happen as a result of your efforts here. First, you'll learn a lot about the various approaches you might urge your lawyer to take. Second, you'll form an opinion as to which of these lawyers you might later turn to if things don't work out with the lawyer you've chosen already. And, probably most importantly, by their professional ethics each of these lawyers, if they've seen you and gained information that is privledged, cannot take your wife's case. So you've closed her out of the top tier, which brings to you an estimable psychological advantage.

There's more.

BAUBLES

Part of getting organized is to keep your mouth shut and start sweating the small stuff for a moment. If you have the benefit of surprise, there are several more ways to use it to your advantage.

JEWELRY:
Gather up all the jewelry that's yours (your family things like grandmother's dinner ring, your father's cufflinks, your spinster aunt's sapphire bracelet, etc.) and what you can lay your hands on of the expensive things you gave her. Make a careful list of what is there. And take it straight to your lawyer's office for safe-keeping.

MAKE SURE THESE ARE SAFE FROM THE VENGEFUL EX:

- Your favorite shotguns.
- Your favorite dog.
- Your favorite sports car.
- Your favorite cufflinks.
- Your favorite putter.
- Your favorite trophies.
- Your favorite guitar.
- Your favorite photo albums (particularly the one of you and the guys fly fishing… *"see, Judge, he was **always** away drinking with his pals…")*.
- As many pictures as you can find of you with the kids (*"It was awful, Judge! He was never with the kids and me…"*).
- The boat keys.
- The King Air keys.
- Anything she knows you love.

Your lawyer's going to have to get it appraised anyway, so she might as well put it in her safe or in the bank safe deposit box. Why? Because it's remarkable how little things like sapphires and rubies can get mysteriously lost in the shuffle when left in the hands of vengeful ex-wives. And just because she's at fault, if she is, doesn't mean for a moment she won't be vengeful. (Hey, you can always give some or all of it back to her later. But it's better in your hands than hers.) Oh, and you'd better move some of your own valuable stuff out of her reach before she gets served.

ARTWORK/SILVER
While you're at it, get everything else that's small and valuable out of the house and to somewhere safe: silver, guns, stock certificates and even porcelains if they're special.

If you have a fine arts policy, make sure it's complete. Favorite paintings have been known to walk off, and if they're not on the policy, you'll lose full value. At the least take a video camera and hold up today's paper – focus the camera on the date so it's clear exactly when the video was shot. If there's a surprise story in the news that day, like a Supreme Court Justice stepping down, or a famous terrorist apprehended, or an unlikely football team winning the Super Bowl, talk about it from time to time throughout the video, just to ensure the authenticity of the video's date. Then video all the valuable artwork, etc in the house. If it disappears, you might be able to recover something through the courts.

THINGS TO MAKE SURE DISAPPEAR BEFORE SHE GETS A HOLD OF/SUBPOENAS THEM:

➢ Your hard drive, including all emails.
➢ Your address book.
➢ Your family jewelry.
➢ The second set of books (or any other accounting).
➢ Photos of your girlfriend(s) past and present (especially if one had been the nanny).
➢ Anything you might own that could suggest illegal drug use. (No morter and pestel in the bathroom.)
➢ Anything that might suggest that you like kinky sex. (Those fur-lined handcuffs you bought your wife as a Valentines joke 5 years ago.)
➢ Any photos of you appearing to be under the influence.
➢ That Halloween party photo of you dressed as Lady Gaga.

CREDIT CARDS AND JOINT CHECKING ACCOUNTS

You'll know when to cancel the jointly held credit cards. Don't forget. Then go to the bank and pull your half of the balance out of the joint accounts. If there's a joint investment account, do the same thing.

Good form requires you tell her. But, relating to timing, understand that doing so is an open act of war.

COHABITATION

Okay, you caught her in the sack (or got caught in the sack yourself, ahem) then you lined up your ducks as best you could, and – ZOCK!—now you've served her (or she's served you, ahem).

Your lawyer says, "Don't move out of the marital residence." And her lawyer gives her the same advice. This is the drawing of the lines for the battle over the custody of the children. No one likes it, but some are way better at it than others. The ones who succeed are the ones who can (1) hold their tempers, and (2) consistently think strategically.

Now you're sharing a house, but no longer a life, with your wife. And your life has never felt more bizarre. You see her in passing – but now she tries to avoid the kitchen when you're in there, or the billiard room, or the library, or whatever place you happen to be – except when the kids are around. Then she elbows you out of the way to serve them the pancakes you just cooked for them.

If she's the obsessive type, she's probably trying to sneak a peak into your briefcase too, if you've left it unlocked. Or your cell phone. Or your laptop. After X years of marriage, she knows your ways. Now she's using that insider knowledge to find out what you know, what you're up to. Do the obvious, but difficult thing: change your ways. If you used to sleep in, get up and go to work early. If you used to play golf on Sundays, stay home and watch football. Or, better still, knock around with the kids.

Welcome to **cohabitation** – not the variety you joked about with your sweetie in college. This is that lovely time that must pass while the judicial system sorts out who will stay in the house with the kids (the odds are against you, sir, even if you're a monk).

Your lawyer will tell you how long this torture will go on. Hopefully it will not be more than two months to the temporary hearing when the judge will decide who stays in the marital residence, how much child support you'll pay, with whom the children will live, when they visit the other parent, and a number of other more minor matters.

WHAT YOU DO DURING THE TRYING TIME CALLED COHABITATION

- Live like you're under a microscope.
- Sadly watch all but your very best friends run for the doors.
- Focus on the kids.
- Talk to the ex only about the kids and the logistics of their immediate lives, nothing else.
- Don't talk to the kids about the specifics of the divorce, except about how it affects their lives.
- Cook for the family and eat with the kids as often as possible.
- Rest a Bible by your bedside.
- Assume your room, car, and office are bugged.
- After helping the little ones with their homework, read books at home in the evenings.
- Don't go out and do little or no drinking at home.

If you choose to move out, you've basically said, "take the kids." That's okay, if that's what you want, and many do. But if you decide to stay, remember always that if you succeed here, you win big.

Here's what's at stake. Being awarded 50 percent of the children's time on the visitation schedule is a big win for a dad. You continue to see plenty of your children thus you stay involved in their lives. That's a big deal. Moreover, in many states child support is influenced by visitation, which is to say it is correctly assumed by the court that every day the children are with you they cost you money, so the more they're with you the less you pay the ex.

Instead of paying the ex to raise your kids, you do it yourself.

DOUBLE LIFE

If you've got an undiscovered girlfriend, encourage her to visit friends in another state for a while. Try not to see her, unless you want to watch her get discovered and then called in as a witness at the temporary hearing, where she can have the special experience of answering under oath in open court where and when she has had sexual relations with you.

Instead, go to work, go to church, be an all-star dad, and keep your nose clean.

It is particularly important during this period that you not write any emails, leave any posts or voicemail messages or send any tweets or texts that you would not like the judge to see. Because the other side is on your case big time now. And they have not only the power and will to subpoena everything in your life that is tangible (including deposing your friends and business associates), but also potentially the use of some very sophisticated tools that are at their disposal, if they decide to use them.

If you use Facebook or LinkedIn, you may be sure the other side is reading what you are writing there. Consider these vehicles just as your wife's lawyer considers them, as avenues to the Judge, and use them to your advantage by placing there *no ugly stuff* about your wife, or the current situation at home. Instead, take care that your online persona be that of the well-meaning, hard-working, loving dad.

As to what you may consider "private" texts and emails, be aware there is software that can be surreptitiously installed on your BlackBerry or *i*-phone that causes, without your knowledge, all the texts you send or receive to go to another (your wife's lawyer's paralegal's?) phone as well. In the "Survival Gear" section of this book's website, www.gentlemansguidetodivorce.com , there is a link to an online store that sells all sorts of counter-intelligence gear that can help you detect bugs and other surveillance gizmos you think may be being utilized on your wife's behalf.

Here again, get a Cricket-style prepaid phone, guard it closely, and communicate with your lover, mostly via texting, using only the pre-paid phone. Because of caller i.d. considerations, these phones are not for general use by you. Replace the pre-paid phones often, and throw the used-up ones in the river when you're done with them. Take care that your lover does the same. In fact, the best way to handle these phones is for you to buy them with cash two at a time, program in your new number and hers to speed-dial, and then take possession of the old ones for disposal. If you use this phone only for communicating with your lover, as you should, and she does the same, the pre-paid minutes will run out at just about the same time.

Under no circumstances let your kids in range of your girlfriend in advance of the temporary hearing, or else just kiss a favorable outcome to the custody battle good-bye. If by some unhappy coincidence they know her -- like she's your ex-best friend's ex-wife whose kids go to your kids' school, you hound-dog -- then just do your best to keep them apart.

SWEET

You've served her with papers so now she knows you know. She runs to her lawyer and they decide: sweet or sour.

Here's the sweet. You're floored. You've confronted her about her carryings on with what's-his-name, and now she's slipping into that negligee you loved her in and bringing you a rum punch...hey, this is great! You know what comes next!

Sorry my friend, shake the randy thoughts and think about whether or not you live in a no-fault state (a real buzz-kill). This negligee stuff doesn't happen in no fault states. If you live in a "fault" state and she shows up in that sexy chemise, run for your life! She's looking to pull off what's called in legal-speak "**condonation**." In some states, after you catch your spouse having sex outside the marriage, if you have sex with her after that, its condonation – wherein you are presumed to condone her prior actions. Talk to your lawyer about this. In the courtroom it kills the fact that she had sex with someone else. You can't use that information any more and she is now entitled to alimony. Unfair? Maybe. Fact – yes.

A pal of mine, a great chef and story-teller, had gone through the whole litigation for well over a year when the soon-to-be-ex invited him out for dinner to talk about boardroom tactics on a scholarship fund with which she was involved. He weighed about 350 lbs. when he caught his wife with the television executive, and now he was down to a sleek 330 the night of this dinner. He was feeling good. Okay. So he and his wife downed tender osso bucco and drank aged chianti classico at his favorite restaurant, right around the corner from his place. One thing led to another (ah! So sweet!) ... after which she headed straight down to the hospital to have a DNA sample drawn. End of story – condonation achieved. They litigated the whole thing all over again for another year, this time without any fault on her part. And for her efforts she got the 350 pound alimony check each month thereafter.

So, you're living in the same house and your wife -- who you just caught cheating with your kids' tennis coach, Carl -- wants very badly, for utterly non-romantic reasons, to have sex with you. She tries again and again. If you leave the marital residence, your risk is that the **guardian ad litem** will think you've ditched the kids. (The guardian is the person who'll be appointed by the courts to your custody case. His/her job will be to carefully review your kids' situation and make recommendations to the judge on the final custody and visitation arrangements for your very own kids.) But if you stay, the little lady (who was just lovin' ole Carl) is going to say it's like old times ("Judge, my husband and I are like rabbits!"). What now?

There's only one way out. Sleep in the guest room with the twin beds that is furthest from where your estranged wife will sleep, and make yourself comfortable there. You may be there awhile. If you and your lawyer are concerned she'll try to convince the court you had sex with her after the revelation of her unfaithfulness (and you should be), here's what you do. Ask that buddy of yours that she can't stand to sleep for the next few evenings in the other twin bed or on the sofa in the room just outside yours. You know, that guy she has hated since he talked down to her in last year's mixed paddle finals. He's here to testify, if need be, that he kept an eye on you all night and there was no condonation possible. He can come in about 9:00 as the kids are going to bed and have a cigar with you. Let him help himself to the kitchen – and no, he doesn't need to worry about cleaning up after any mess in there. Then in the morning he can stick around for early breakfast with the kids, but go off to work before they go to school. There's no problem about the kids knowing he's there and their being annoyed by it.

You'll drive her crazy and soon she'll decide it's better to "stipulate to no condonation" just to get that S.O.B. out of the house.

Be sure to thank him with the bottle of his favorite bourbon he so richly deserves.

OR SOUR

This is the mother-of-them-all fight.

First and foremost, this woman whose head is spinning like Linda's in *The Exorcist* is not your wife. She may look the same, but she's now under the spell of her closest confidants – her attorney, her friends, perhaps even her mother who always hated you (or so she's now saying). Remember this.

She's picking a real fight – one of those humdingers you see on TV.

1. Be the GENTLEMAN you are.

2. Again, POSITIVELY DO NOT TOUCH her.

3. Keep as cool and controlled as you possibly can. You will potentially hear everything you say - exaggerated - in the courtroom. Don't talk about yourself. And don't talk about her. (Do you really want to hear your voice – wow, she was recording that?? – in open court saying that she's a bad kisser and you never liked her ass in pants?) Be a gentleman and talk only about what's best for the children.

4. If you can, secretly record this "conversation" on the little recorder or BlackBerry in your pocket. That recording may come in handy later – you'll be floored at what she may say to you (wouldn't you rather have *her* voice played back in the courtroom saying she never liked *your* ass in pants?)

5. Did I mention be a gentleman?

6. UNDERSTAND THAT THIS IS AN ARGUMENT THAT CANNOT BE WON – it's simply meant to make you angry enough to say some useful things for *her* hidden recorder, or to make you take a swing at her (see The Cops). Her objective is to make you be the monster she wants to convince the court you are.

7. Let her vent. (You may well find that the calmer you are the more crazy she becomes.)

8. NO MATTER WHAT: try to keep any hateful talk away from the ears of the children. This is the scene they'll be recalling to their spouse or shrink in 2030.

THE COPS

Family Court judges don't like lawbreakers any more than Criminal Court judges do.

Nothing would please the ex and her lawyer more than you, on the eve of the temporary hearing, getting into trouble with the law. Nothing. This prospect is so appealing that out of the blue, one night while you are cohabitating, the ex may try to pick another fight with you, especially if she and her lawyer don't feel they got all they needed the first time.

You'll know this is what's going on because this time she'll go chin to chin with you. Get ready:
> She'll tell you graphically what a lousy lover you were.
> She'll tell you how she's hated you for years because of some incident that chafed her raw a long time ago.
> She'll be horrible about your mother, or family.
> She'll call your girlfriend (if you have one she knows about) a whore.

She wants you to take a swing at her. DON'T DO IT. She may even grab you in the hopes you'll scratch her or bruise her as you try to get away from her. Don't react. Even so, she will probably call the cops. Here's how to handle them.

> Be completely and utterly calm, so much so that your voice is barely above a whisper.
> Say repeatedly that you didn't touch her, that you never have or would.

➢ Explain to them that this is a difficult time and she's under a lot of pressure, and her lawyer clearly told her to call 911 and report a criminal domestic violence incident, even though there wasn't one...which there wasn't. You might even tell them she's been talking about doing this to get you to move out of the house.
➢ Promise them you'll go back into the house and straight to your room and you won't see her any more that evening.

When the cops leave, wait for the house to go to sleep, then pack your bag and get out of there. She's too psycho to share a house with (and this behavior is horrible for the kids). If you stay she'll probably do it again and this time you'll land in the cooler. The cops don't like coming back and back and back just to give a warning. Warnings wear thin fast. Their attitude will soon be to let the judge sort it out.

Now it's okay to leave the kids. The judge and the guardian will understand she's crazy and acting on the recommendations of her counsel, and you can't stay in a house where someone's calling the cops on you.

The good news is when you're staying at the club, the bar – and maybe a buddy or two -- are right downstairs from the rooms.

KIDS 1

The divorce is clearly in the works -- you may be living in the same house, but nearly everything else has changed – and the kids know it.

The toughest part about divorce is its effect emotionally, socially, and financially on the kids. Some parents are sensitive about this and carefully walk this minefield together to ensure the best result for their children. But you're in the nasty divorce, so what's right for the kids is coming in a distant second to your soon-to-be ex's perceived needs. In nasty divorces the battle for the kids is more a battle for the money – the more time she gets with the kids, the more child support she gets from you. She'll be a nutcase about getting custody if she's been caught in an affair in a fault state so under state law *can't* get alimony. Any involvement of the kids is wrong, but some is virtually inevitable. Just remain a gentleman and you'll get through it.

Kids are smart and they are naturally sympathetic to the weaker parent, which initially is probably their mother. Expect this and don't let it get to you. Over time they become fairer-minded and then when the ex starts shredding you, they'll come to your defense.

If she's really insecure (this is bad), desperate (this is worse), mean (horrors!), or vindictive (horror of horrors!), she'll try to turn the kids against you. She'll do this by trying to appeal to their insecurities at this time. The shrewdest ex's won't say these evil things directly to the kids. Instead, to ensure maximum shock effect, they'll unload to a trusted friend, for example, or to a mother who has temporarily moved in, but *within earshot of the children*. This way the children can hear this creepy stuff clearly without having to respond to it, or discuss it. It can just fester.

In the heat of their campaigns to win the affirmative votes of their children, psycho ex-wives say things like:

Dad's a liar. He always lies.

If Dad gets his way, the kids'll never see their Mom again.

Dad doesn't like their friends. He doesn't even know their names.

Dad doesn't like their dog. He's never even fed him.

Dad's mean, and he's being mean to her.

Dad's trying to take the kids away from her.

Dad doesn't understand them or even try to, only she does.

She's going to be very poor because Dad is keeping all the money. He's stealing her money and the children's too.

Only she can take care of the children when they're sick, hurt, etc.

Dad didn't go to all their plays, games, etc – and she did.

Dad didn't put together their birthday parties – she did.

Dad's always on the phone/computer/etc. – he's not there for them.

At this point the court has assigned – with yours and your wife's mutual consent -- a person to make recommendations to the judge about what's best for your kids: the **guardian ad litem**. This person's job is to ensure the best interests of the children. Guardians, who may be attorneys, are well-meaning and have a difficult job – especially when the kids are being fed the lines your ex is feeding yours. To them "the best interests of the children" is the gold standard. In some states this role is played by a **custody evaluator** who may be a psychologist.

It's important to remember the guardian has probably seen just about everything. In the case before yours, the Hatfields and the McCoys are lined up in front of the kids and are slinging insults at one another. And in the case following yours, drunken dad is pointing a butcher knife at mom and advancing on her and the kids. Or maybe it's the case of the mom who caught her husband with her sister and after beating her sister with a sawed-off garden hose (metal tip and all) she went at dad – who had hidden in the kids' room. As crazy as you may think your life has become, to the guardian your situation is like an all expenses paid afternoon at the country club.

The guardian's job is mostly to try to figure out who's being honest. In light of that, keep in mind that many of the things you do now will end up on paper on the guardian's desk -- and that'll be the basis of a recommendation to the judge. (Note: the judge takes the guardian's recommendations very seriously – it's his only unbiased window into the kids' lives.)

Here's what you do:
> Talk with your kids. Understand your kids' lives and discuss what's happening.
> Figure out how what's happening is affecting them. Then try to make it better.
> Answer their questions. Try to reduce their angst.
> Difficult as it may be, don't say anything bad about their mom to them.
> Hug them and kiss them often. They are now your closest relatives.
> Watch them closely for signs of their acting out.
> If they need help, get it for them.
> Remember your ex is trying to make you into a monster, which makes discipline very tricky. If you speak harshly or worse, spank one of the children, that'll get straight back to the guardian. Be careful how you handle disciplining the kids.

If the divorce is especially nasty, chances are the guardian will introduce a child psychologist into the arena to determine how the kids are faring. In some cases, if the children are young and their mother is especially good at mind games, the ex will convince the kids even to lie to the therapist because they're afraid they'll lose Mommy. This is terribly sad, but not to be feared. It's just part of the evil chess game of a nasty divorce. Be completely honest and open with the therapist about what you think is going on on the other side, and then encourage the therapist to talk with the child alone. Chances are the therapist will find inconsistencies in the child's stories and dig deeper into what's really going on.

Don't fear the truth. A brilliant kid can't fool the average child psychologist (who's seen a lot) for long.

Another thing to be aware of: you will notice that, especially in the early months of your separation, the children are unsettled and perhaps somewhat more poorly behaved than usual when they first arrive at your house from their mother's, and also just before they leave to go back to their mother's. Psychologists call these times "transitions." Mom's house and Dad's house have different rules, and they're just trying to process that.

Be especially forgiving of children acting up during transitions. For example, if Junior gets dropped off from school on Thursday afternoon and he struts into your house acting like a wise ass, give him a little space. Turn on your favorite Bill Evans tune and unload the dishwasher. Let the cool in the music have a turn at him.

AFFIDAVITS

In cases where the custody of the children is at issue, immediately after the divorce has been filed, your lawyer will ask you to help get affidavits from your friends and associates. These sworn testimonials are intended to showcase what a good dad you are, and sometimes what a lousy mom your ex is. They will also indicate the general direction of these potential witnesses' respective testimonies throughout the trial.

In my opinion, this is the lowest point of all.

Now you'll learn who your real friends are. And chances are, if in fact you have been a good guy and your ex was misbehaving, there will be new people you never thought of who are angry with your ex for what she did. You'll start hearing about things that previously were concealed from you. Be ready, some of what you'll hear might make you really angry.

Some pointers:
- ➤ Try to convince friends who are equally friendly with your wife and you to stay neutral by filing no affidavit.
- ➤ Try to convince your friends that putting in an affidavit now may very well prevent them from having to give a **deposition** later.
- ➤ If there's anyone you know who doesn't like the ex, sound that person out about what he/she might be willing to swear to about her lousy character.
- ➤ Try to recall all the former maids, housekeepers, babysitters and other household employees, and then do your best to find the ones who were strong personalities and interview them. You may find some fertile ground here.

- ➤ Don't forget the girls in the exercise class. They know all. They have opinions. And if yours is a high profile divorce, they'll LOVE being involved and having something to talk about.
- ➤ Line up as many of your friends as you can. They know what a great dad you are. Don't forget the headmaster at the school, especially if you've been a reliable giver.

Now you'll also learn who your real enemies are. Because the ex is working hard on her affidavits as well.

Brace yourself for the bilge water that'll be spewed out by the rats she drags in. You won't recognize yourself.

THE TEMPORARY HEARING

All that has come before is the lead up to the Temporary Hearing. Here's where the judge will determine who temporarily stays in the house, who has temporary custody of the children, what the near-term visitation schedule will be, and what you're going to be paying on a monthly basis to keep the ship afloat, even though the likelihood is you will no longer be living on board.

This is the hearing where your lawyer will want to trip up the ex and, if he can, catch her in an apparent lie. For example, you might get the family prescription medication records from the local pharmacy. Several years back the ex might have had some trouble with fear of flying so the doctor prescribed Valium. Maybe she had it filled, but never took one pill. Or maybe she took them all. In your affidavits, your side will present the fact that the ex has been prescribed these pills, and that she had the prescription filled. There are the pharmacy records right there. In most states the divorcing couple doesn't answer questions directly at the Temporary Hearing, they don't take the witness stand. But your ex's attorney will want to deflect this hot topic for her. They won't want the judge to think she could be knocked out on barbiturates when she's supposed to be caring for the children. So they'll have to come up with an excuse, hopefully without much chance to think it over. How does it sound? Does it fly?

Then there's the DUI from when she was in college. Or the parents who were going to sue because she let their kid ride a bike on a dirt road and he rolled it over on his head into a ditch. What? She didn't even make the kid wear a helmet? What do you have to say for yourself, ma'am?

This is her rap sheet as a mother. How does it look, and how does her side look trying to defend it?

They will seek to trick you too, of course. This is a high stakes game and the sword cuts both ways.

The time will go quickly at this hearing, but the dirty looks from the ex across the courtroom will be slow to fade from your memory. As with any competition, the worse your opponent looks the worse she's doing. If she looks like she's playing bridge with the girls, you're losing. But that's unlikely. It is much more likely the look you'll see in her, whom you know so well, will be that of desperation – or vindictiveness.

Watch your wallet and remember Sir Isaac.

JUDGES

Family Court dockets are full up and it takes a while to get a hearing. As with the rest of the judicial system, it seems there are more cases than judges to hear them.

When your divorce is first filed, the Temporary Hearing will be placed before the first judge who's available. You and your lawyer will probably have little control over who this judge may be. The Clerk of Court will probably just assign someone on the basis of their being in the right courthouse with a half day open on their schedule 30-60 days from the date of filing.

There's a lot more discretion when the time comes for your final hearing judge to be assigned. This is the judge who will become familiar with the details of your case and who will hear the arguments upon which his **Final Order** (your divorce decree) is based.

Some of my best friends are judges. Judges come in all shapes and sizes. They are not all Boy Scouts. Relevant to Family Court matters, some Family Court judges have been through the system themselves. I know one who was caught in a fault state cheating on his wife.

Who wouldn't want that guy if you were caught cheating?

An experienced Family Court lawyer knows the personal lives of the judges, what sorts of decisions they have rendered in the past in cases where discretion was allowed, and what are their pet peeves. This is what lawyers talk about around the courthouse and at the water cooler. An experienced Family Court lawyer serves his client very well by seeking to match up your case with the most sympathetic judge. Typically this is done through your lawyer's paralegal who is working with the Clerk of Court on scheduling the first hearing. Her task is a delicate one that she performs by knowing which judge is sitting when and refusing the court dates offered by the Clerk until she knows the right judge is sitting.

Some judges admire sports heroes. Others dislike lawyers. Since they are either elected or, more likely, appointed by elected officials, judges are politically sensitive. The smart client asks about the various judges who are available and urges his lawyer to bring the case before the most sympathetic judge.

Go judge-shopping. And don't look back.

Reporters

The details of broken relationships are best left in the courtroom. Unfortunately, the better known the combatants, the less likely this is to be the case. Adults are adults and in general they can handle it, although, depending on what they do and the details to be proffered, their careers may take a hit. The part that's tough is when the children learn about their parents' divorce from other kids on the playground. These painful and unnecessary memories are slow to fade.

In truth, what goes on in a courtroom is almost always public information. Judges can say they will "seal" a settlement, "in the best interests of the children," but if a news outlet is willing to go to court to get it, overwhelmingly they will succeed.

It is what goes on outside the courtroom where control can be exercised.

When public people squabble, there are many who will pay for a front row seat. It is axiomatic: the bigger the names, the more who will be interested. The magazines at the supermarket check-out make a market trafficking in this sort of information, and when the hard facts run short they get creative with the soft stuff. These fish-wrappers' – to a greater or lesser extent, depending upon the publication -- stock in trade is to take a relatively commonplace comment and twist it into an unrecognizable sensation. The best of their editors are the ones who do this with the most imaginative flair.

Tabloid reporters and editors – some of whom are friends of mine -- don't so much make stuff up as twist the things they are told into spicier, more sensational copy.

What they do is most easily avoided by simply not taking their phone calls. However, sometimes my friends are authorized by their editors to offer real checks in exchange for real information, or for that which passes for real information.

The savvy gentleman and his lawyer make it their business to be familiar with the financial situations and moral turpitude of all who are in a position to know the potentially damaging details of the case. Some, such as lawyers, doctors, psychologists and judges, are barred by professional ethics from speaking publicly about private matters. That helps, but it is barely reliable. What newspaper hasn't sold extra copies hawking leaked grand jury testimony?

Ex-wives, ex-girlfriends, ex-caddies, ex-captains and even housekeepers, gardeners and private tennis instructors are not similarly constrained.

When discretion falters only money ensures silence. This legalized blackmail is called the **confidentiality agreement**, a little trust fund that can be yanked for cause and whose beneficiary is the secret-keeper. If you enter into one, do not pay a single lump sum. Instead, offer the steady trickle that is just a bit more than what the tabloids will pay. Thus it is important, if sometimes humbling, to know what bad news about you might be worth. Friendly reporters, editors and big-city PR guys can get you a round number.

There was a day when a studio executive could say, "If you do that to me, you'll never eat lunch in this town again." In recent years, the internet has sufficiently diffused power over communications such that this line can no longer be used with confidence.

The only reliable gag today is grease. And if you look in the right places, there are tubs of it in use.

Moving Out

You've endured the cohabitation (or not) and you've finally arrived at the time to hear what the judge has to say.

You're out. #!%$@*! Now what?

Moving to a furnished apartment or house somewhere near the kids is preferable. But taking half the furniture out of the house where your children continue to live just two months after they've first learned of their parents' impending divorce? That might go at the Two Bits Trailer Park, but not on Summit Street.

If the judge decides it's the ex who's leaving the marital residence, brace yourself. That's good, but whether she's allowed to or not, she's taking a bunch of stuff with her. Somehow the system is predicated upon the notion that stuff is more important to women than men, and that women are therefore entitled to more of it. This does not mean that in the final accounting, all the stuff (that can be found) isn't accounted for and assigned a value and each of you get your fair share of that value.

Now comes what we'll call The Divorce Attorney Playbook 101's suggestion that will drive you crazy. The ex's lawyer will tell her to get as much as she can out of the house – without you there. There's a lot of value in furniture, artwork, silver, etc, and many a man has come home to find nothing but bare light bulbs and a mattress when the ex moves out. Part of the effectiveness of this plan is that in the rush things like sapphires can fall through the cracks (this is why you locked them up at your lawyer's). They're also counting on the fact that you didn't prepare for this by being organized and accounting on paper/video/photo for much or all of the valuable stuff in the house -- that you were too busy being you to take stock.

The play works like this: the guardian will suggest to you correctly and sincerely that it would be in the best interests of the children to make sure that they are out of the house when mom packs up, and you'll probably want to take them on a little trip. There'll be an agreement between the lawyers (or it may even be stipulated in the Judge's **Temporary Order)** that "the wife can remove from the marital residence only her personal and business-related items." Be aware no good turn goes unpunished. As you and the kids are driving off to the airport for a weekend of skiing to get them out of the house while the ex is getting her few things out, an enormous moving van is driving into town with your address on its GPS.

If the ex is moving out, find a way to catalog what she's taking because all this stuff has to be accounted for later. (Again, here's where a video of each room's contents can help a lot. A true inventory list drawn up by a local appraiser is far preferable.)

Playbook moves aside, the guardian is correct, Moving Day is really scary for the kids, not to mention that it's an emotional day for the parents. If they can be reasonable at all, the parents should work together to find a way for the kids to be out of the house when the movers are there.

You, sir, must be reasonable as well. You have shared this house with your ex for some time. The house won't look the same, *some* stuff has to go with her (or you) and in the end chances are you'll split it half and half. Don't resent what's going out as long as it's reasonable.

Last thought on this: once you're out, you're out. Don't expect her to welcome you back in to pick up forgotten items. Take all your personal stuff and don't look back – this isn't your house any more. Whatever got left, if you ever see it again, is a bonus.

Now you understand why the jewels are in your lawyer's safe.

KIDS 2

Whether you're still staying in the old family manse or not, your relationship with your children just entered a new phase. Now *they're* in charge. Their mom wants you to be a monster and if she's playing them as part of the nasty-divorce-custody-fight, you've lost a lot of authority for the time being. You can't say no or "because I said so" to them anymore. If you do, they may go crying to their mom or to the guardian and then you'll have the guardian on your case asking a bunch of questions and implicitly threatening to take your kids away from you.

Here's your best bet:
Remember, this is temporary -- and important. There isn't anything fair about it – it's just plain the way it is. The more you want to keep your kids, the better you'll be at this.

> - Get a widescreen HD television and set it up in the biggest room in the house with a bunch of comfortable club chairs and a refrigerator full of soda pop in the corner. Get the cool surround sound home theatre sound system. (When the kids aren't around, you can watch it too.)
> - Hire a tutor to help them with their homework (DON'T let their grades slip on your watch. Plus, it's good for their egos to excel in school during this tough time.)
> - If you can't cook, learn! (Read my *Cooking Guide* for a lot that was hard-won about cooking for the kids, and a variety of other aspects of custody battle strategies.) It's easy, if you try. If you won't learn, get a cook so the meals around the place improve.
> - If you are not able to take them yourself, hire the coolest responsible kid in town to take the kids to and from school.

- Don't let them get bored at your house – come up with fun things to do with them. Go bowling, to the beach, to movies, to a pro baseball/football/soccer game.
- Go to oddball places like the stockyards, or an auto auction, or a tent revival, but make sure the children are rested, their stomachs are full and they've got water when they get there. Then see the scene and get out before they start griping.
- Indulge yourself a little here and subtly build the children's respective self esteems too. Up to now you haven't told them much about their forefathers. Maybe that's because there never seemed to be the right time, or maybe you didn't know enough. Well now you do. Learn about your children's great-great-grandparents, even if it's just a shred. Put the best face on what you've learned and talk to your children about them. This is image building and it is to replace at least in part the lost self-image of once being the cozy child of two loving parents. Plus it makes sense. In the days before the separation the ex was always there and there was other stuff to talk about besides Great Uncle Fred the Indian Fighter. But now it's just me and I dig Great Uncle Fred. Or, if it's daughters you have at the table, then how about your great grandmother Matilda the society dame on Beacon Hill who put a minie ball through an intruder's gizzard? Talk to them about who they are. Build them up. Have some fun with it. If they're American teen-agers, they'll act like they hate it. Soldier on. They'll hear every story, repeat it to their friends tomorrow, and remember it forever!
- If mom never let them have a dog and you always wanted one, now's the time to get that hound (as long as you can handle him). Keep in mind that the kids will love playing with him, but you're stuck with Rex when they head over to the ex's. Choose the breed carefully: mellow kid-lovers such as labs, Golden Retrievers, and Norwegian Mountain Dogs are great. Oh, and make sure your kids aren't allergic BEFORE you get the dog.

Why are you doing all this? Because regularly now the court-appointed guardian will be speaking with each of the children on the telephone (you'll see the calls on her bills) and the major questions she'll be asking them are "How are you doing at Mom's house?" and "How's it going at Dad's house?"

There are some DO NOT's associated with this phase as well.

> DO NOT cave to your seven-year-old daughter's every whim: if she really wants a kitten and you hate cats, the kitten is no cuter when your daughter is gone than when she's there.
> DO NOT let your sons do crazy things like riding motorcycles or skydiving on your watch. Sending them to mom busted up doesn't fly.
> DO NOT take them on trips that might be considered in any way dangerous. One of my more exuberant pals, thinking they'd think he was cool, took his teenage kids to Cuba – illegally. Imagine how that went over with the ex, and of course the guardian and the judge. Not cool.
> DO NOT let the 16 or 17 year-olds drink. Some dads think it's okay if they are at home (the he's-safer-here-than-out-on-the-road reasoning). Try explaining that choice to the guardian.
> DO NOT load all the homework on mom. When the word gets to the custody evaluator that the children don't have to do their homework at Dad's house, there will be consequences that are unfortunate for you.
> DO NOT let the children and their friends just sit around your house watching television. Similarly, when the custody evaluator gets that picture she's going to conclude that the healthier environment – the one where the parent is more positively involved – is at mom's. Not Good.
> When it's time for the kids to go to mom's, DO NOT send them home dirty, wet, sunburned, cold, or even hungry if you can help it. *("My poor babies, what HAS he done to you now?")*

For this short period, if you have teenagers, go ahead and let there be an element of *Animal House* in your house – but don't you be John Belushi and NO food fights.

WWTGS … (What would the guardian say?) is your mantra during this period.

EERIE ECHOES

When the kids say, "Mom says you're stealing/lying/taking/hiding" whatever from her or them, don't answer Mom directly through them. Just deal with the facts as they are alleged. Whatever you do, don't be defensive – the kids will think you're hiding something or trying to get away with something that you're not. It's easy to want to counter-attack mom along with her allegations – but it makes you appear defensive. Instead, calmly dissolve each allegation by quietly and confidently revealing the facts.

Or, the same game played more subtly. There may come a time when all of a sudden the children care about things they never cared about before, especially material things like charm bracelets or cufflinks, or better still, stocks and bonds. The first time you hear it you do a double-take. *The kid who last week forgot his $250 skis back at the lodge is all of a sudden sweating it about the mother-of-pearl cufflinks his grandmother gave him?*

As you instruct the custodian to pay your daughter's tuition (which you have always done) from the UGMA account you set up for her education (with *your* money years ago), *your daughter suddenly says you're "stealing" her money.*

Take it head on. Explain to your daughter (if she's older than, say, 14) that she is entitled to an accounting of every dollar in the account. Tell her you'll set up a one-on-one meeting with her and the money manager (or the custodian, if he's scarier) so that she can go through the expenditures line-by-line.

Find the cufflinks and call the lad away from his favorite television show to discuss with him at length where they were, and where he might put them now, so that he can more readily keep track of them. He'll probably ask you to watch them for him. Whatever, just have some fun with it.

What's happening here? The ex is hearing from her lawyer that a potential fertile line of attack will be to make you into a crook. And what's lower than a father stealing from his kids? The ex now has this lowlife stuff in her head and she's using the children to be her gumshoes.

Since they've been put up to this work, their hearts are not entirely in it. This means if you play your part correctly, they'll give theirs up fast.

Or, it may be that the ex is loaded, and perhaps you're less so. These exs love to imagine themselves the victims of predators … like you. She gives young Harry $15 to buy you a Christmas present, but foolishly he spends $20 on a pocket knife you once suggested to him was a nice one. He goes to her for the extra $5.

Now you're "using" the boy to "steal" her money.

Be assured the children will soon tire of their new law enforcement role – particularly when it becomes clear that mom is often falsely on an attack mode rampage about this. And dad's clean. When they connect those dots, it may well begin to turn the tide. That's where their efforts to defend/protect mom might turn into a defense of dad – and their experience may cause them to think a little less of mom and a little more of dad.

Hey. But who's counting?

THE CLUB

Half of all American marriages end in divorce these days. The number is even higher among more affluent Americans. Accordingly, statistically, there are a half dozen guys at the club going through what you're going through right now.

Except in the case of your very best friends, they don't want to hear stories of your psycho ex-wife and you don't want to hear about theirs. So keep what's going on to yourself and hope they do the same.

Whether they mean to or not, guys in the thick of divorces and custody fights hang together – they may not talk about it, but they're in a fraternity of sorts. When a stranger walks into the restaurant they're in and sits down alone, one fraternity brother may glance at another – perhaps from as far apart as across the room – and mouth "P.I.". There are knowing glances between them that say "she's got the plague" when somebody's sue-him-to-smithereens ex walks through the club. On the golf course a private plane flies over low. *"Now she's got the AWACs out,"* one pal mutters. The nice thing about knowing the other guys are there is the reminder that even though you are going through something quite personal, there are others suffering a similar experience. Then somehow you know you're going to be okay. You're all going to survive this tough time.

With the simple understanding of keeping your mouth shut about the details of your divorce, the club is great now. You'll never appreciate it more. Clubs were invented for single guys. Work on your squash or tennis or backgammon game. You can whack with great fury that little ball, and the effectiveness of your game may well improve with the fury of your stroke. If you're a shotgunner, a round or two of sporting clays can also rejuvenate, although the skeet field heats up the barrel faster. At the gym, you've finally got the time and the inclination to punch through to the next level.

Then there's the networking. If you need a forensic accountant, the club's a great place to get a lead on a good one. You want good tickets to the ballgame so your teenager can bring a friend? Put out the word around the club. You want your seven-year-old to catch a couple of big trout over the weekend before the meeting he just told you he has next week with the guardian? The club's stocked stream is just the place – or someone there at the club will know just the spot where even a kid can hook a few big boys.

In the spirit of getting back into the groove, the club is a great place for camaraderie and release, not to mention somebody may just have a sister in town. But no matter what, it's best not to hang out in the bar. Guardians have unknown networks, and while a DUI is never good, in the middle of a custody battle getting one will surely be devastating.

One last tip: avoid gambling, and slip out of the bar or party before the night howlers ramp up.

The Gym

The doctors will tell you to go to the gym to release endorphins and relieve stress at this stressful time.

Not this doctor. You're handling the stress just fine.

In the days after becoming separated you will find that your new routine provides you with blocks of time you used not to have. Sure you've got homework to do to find all the things your lawyer's paralegal needs. But you've still got time, and the gym provides you a way to get out into your community for a low risk look around. Don't be shy. Self-improvement is always a good thing. So is information-gathering.

Go to the gym to get buff and check out the ladies. You may have forgotten by now the earlier chapter entitled "Brazilian." A point of that chapter is when women are looking around for new guys, they do predictable things, among which is to go to the gym to get toned up.

When they asked John Dillinger why he robbed banks, he replied sensibly, "Because that's where the money is."

So who's at the gym? Toned up women looking for guys.

While you're there get to know the trainers. They can tell you who's looking, maybe they'll even play a little Cupid. One nuance: do not try to pick up women at the gym. That's creepy and it rarely works. Instead determine who interests you, where they work, who their friends are, etc, and then pursue independent channels for the effective approach.

Just ask a couple of innocent questions like "Who's that?" and you'll be amazed how much information comes back. The gym crowd gossips as much as does the beauty parlor crowd. If you worked all day in a gym, what would you be talking about? And with all those mirrors around, how could you not be narcissistic?

Importantly, unlike traditional beauty parlors where information is exchanged freely among relative strangers, guys can go to gyms.

Just one caution: When you go, listen. But watch what you say. Do not say one word you wouldn't want the judge to hear.

THE TRACK

It is okay to sit in the Trustee's Box at the track with your kids and watch your horses run. It's a little less okay to sit in the Trustee's Box and watch your friends' horses run. It's least okay to sit in the grandstand alone and watch anyone's horses run. It is flat out *not* okay to be out in the grandstand and passing to and from the betting windows.

Look, Vegas is out – suffice to say, it's not a family place if you're not there with the family. And some other spots are out too.

TOP 10 PLACES TO BE SEEN DURING A CUSTODY BATTLE:

1. Church.
2. Parent-teacher conference.
3. Sunday School.
4. Parents' Association meeting.
5. Children's horse show.
6. Grocery store buying organic milk and potato chips.
7. Pick-up line at school.
8. Kids soccer game.
9. Kids birthday party.
10. CPR class.

TOP 10 PLACES NOT TO BE SEEN AT THIS POINT IN YOUR CUSTODY BATTLE:

1. Any hotel lobby with your best friend's (or boss's) wife.
2. Vegas.
3. Harry's Bar – every night. Alone.
4. Any nude beach.
5. With the girlfriend from before your marriage - the one your wife hated and always brought up during arguments.
6. Any gay bar holding hands with your son's chess coach, Victor.
7. Getting pierced – ear, nose, tongue, nipple. No holes, thanks.
8. Chatting with the high school cheerleaders – if your daughter isn't one.
9. Shopping for a new Porsche/Jaguar/Donzie.
10. Huddled in a corner of an adult bookstore (worse, theater).

The string is pretty short nowadays on what you can and should be doing. As long as the custody battle is going on, getting back into the groove comes with limitations.

GIRLFRIENDS

If you didn't enjoy the company of women, you wouldn't be in this mess.

Your life is being conducted now under a microscope. If your adultery caused the break-up, you'll be well served to keep your girlfriend(s) under wraps and out of the news.

The same goes if it *wasn't* your adultery and the girlfriend came along after the break-up.
Whatever. Let's just say there's a girlfriend somewhere out there.

Here's the thing about girlfriends. If the divorce gets to a final hearing, the chances are your girlfriend will be called as a witness somewhere along the way. If the trial's being covered by the press, the girlfriend can add some luster to the proceedings, but otherwise her appearance on the stand at the final hearing isn't really anything to be feared.

More than one girlfriend becomes, as you might imagine, considerably more problematic. Just a reminder: like wives, girlfriends like to be the only one, and when they find they're not, they can be unpleasant and unpredictable about it, and you. Now she becomes a potential witness for the ex -- and that is definitely to be feared.

TYPES OF GIRLFRIENDS TO STEER CLEAR OF AT THIS POINT:

➤ Avoid the girl with tattoos (OK, maybe one little one) or multiple piercings.
➤ Avoid anyone married. (duh.)
➤ Avoid the aggressive pursuer. (duh.)
➤ Avoid anyone with a malicious side (don't worry, you'll be able to see it) – she could quickly have you over a barrel, turning your situation to her advantage.
➤ Absolutely avoid criers. (Haven't you had enough?)
➤ Absolutely avoid screamers. (What are you, a masochist?)
➤ Avoid anyone in the office. (Do you want two ex's in your life right now?)
➤ Absolutely avoid anyone clearly searching for commitment. (Chances are the first girl off the blocks for you isn't the one. But if she thinks you're the one for her…then you're in for it.)
➤ Avoid the angry type. (If you really want to get spanked, just wait until you see your lawyer's bills.)

SOME MORE GIRLFRIEND POINTERS:

1.   Keep the girlfriend away from the children, even at church. Guardians don't like girlfriends. You're supposed to be hanging with the kids during this difficult time, and girlfriends inevitably take dads away from their kids.

2.   Another reason to keep the kids away from the girlfriend: kids talk and they're going to tell their mom about Dad's new girlfriend. And mom's going to be scrupulous about seeing (spinning/inventing) the worst, and passing it along to the guardian.

3.   By all means get a girlfriend, but try to get it right the first time.

You'd do it even if I told you not to.

WILD CARDS:
VISITATION, CUSTODY, AND MORE

Unfortunately for all of us, when it comes to the topic at hand either I or friends of mine have made just about every mistake you can imagine. One that comes to mind here is my frugal friend who decided he'd rely on his friend the real estate attorney as sole legal counsel for his divorce. A happily married-to-his-first-wife guy with no background whatsoever in family law, the real estate attorney friend basically agreed to walk into the courtroom with my pal and warm the lawyer's chair in exchange for my pal letting the real estate attorney go deer hunting on my friend's ranch. That was a deal!

If my friend had needed a closing schedule, that might have worked.

But a **visitation schedule**? No way.

What's a visitation schedule? Good question, the real estate attorney didn't know either, and between the two of them, these deer-skinners managed to get "visitation," "physical custody" and "custody" all mixed up.

Custody is the determination by the Court of who will be the decision-maker on where the children go to school, who will make the final call if there are medical decisions for a child that must be made, and if the children have assets of their own, how those assets will be managed. **Joint custody** is very common, meaning the parents have to agree on these decisions, although in the case of an impasse, one is given 51% for particular decisions and the other has 51% for others. (In other words, in the case of an impasse, final decision goes to say, Dad regarding financial matters, or to Mom for health matters, or Dad for education decisions, etc. All this ends up in the Final Order.)

Visitation is simply where the kids stay and when they stay there, which parent gets them on which holiday, what portion of what vacation and so forth. Guardians and judges know dozens of visitation schedules, schedules to meet most every situation.

Since my friend traveled a lot in his job and couldn't raise the kids day-to-day, and since he didn't know the difference between custody and visitation, he agreed to give away full custody. Down the line, the effect of that confusion was that the vindictive ex happily found herself in charge of the money my frugal friend (for tax-avoidance purposes) had given his kids. She was entitled to make all the decisions as to where they should go to school, and when the kids needed money for schools or medical bills or clothes or plane fares. In other words she was entitled for many years to make unilateral cash calls on my friend.

The old timers know you can go back to court to get visitation changed if there's a "change of circumstance." Custody's tougher to get changed after the fact, by which I mean the parent with custody would have, for example, to get convicted of a crime, or disappear, or become certifiably crazy to lose custody once it has been gained. And going back to court carries with it the costs of filing fees, at least, and of course legal fees. Accordingly, my frugal friend has so far refused to go back to court to get these mistakenly-imposed wrongs righted.

You probably don't need a great lawyer, but when the open-ended cash pit we know as our children are involved, it's worth the price to get a lawyer who's been around the block enough to have learned how to read the street signs.

THE FINAL HEARING

If you're lucky, this final act will come quickly, perhaps as soon as a year after the divorce proceedings were initiated. But chances are it won't be that fast.

Whatever else you're doing and no matter how much you dislike the situation, take the time to understand your case. In particular understand the nuances of the property settlement you are seeking and why, under the law, your side's theory is defensible.
You will be asked to testify. If you don't know what you're doing, you could easily cost yourself a boatload of cash.

Don't be hateful. In fact you may find it helpful – as a way of staying dispassionate – not to look at the ex, to try to just forget she's there. Your attitude should be "This is just business."

The judge will get to know you during this experience and you want him to think you're a nice guy who is a good, responsible and caring father. Yes, he has a Guardian's Final Report, and that's important. But the judge's word is the final word and it will be substantially affected by his impression of you.

Let her be the drama queen, you be Steady Eddie.

Trust your lawyer. He or she is privy to a lot of privileged information. There will, for example, be conferences when the judge will call the lawyers into his chambers and try various scenarios out on them. Ask your lawyer what was said in these conferences as it may affect the direction of your testimony. He's not supposed to tell you, but if you have a good relationship, he'll make sure you know what you need to know.

Agree with your lawyer on a strategy and both of you stick to it. If revelations cause a change in strategy, take a break and agree on the best new direction. Only a chucklehead lies to his lawyer.

Of course don't lie on the stand either, which is known as perjury. Things go bad fast when the judge starts to think you're not telling the truth. You do not, however, have to tell all you know. Answer the questions the ex's lawyer asks you narrowly. You can be less guarded when it is your lawyer asking the questions. In general, the less you say the better will be the outcome for you. So don't get it into your head to show off.

This is the time you've been waiting for – an ending to the madness. Don't get ahead of yourself. These days are some of the most important days of your divorce.

Her Stuff

As much as you dislike moving, one day you will move out of the marital residence that you shared with your ex – it's funny how new wives don't really like the house you and your ex picked out back in 'the day.' Your new wife sees the house as "her" (that is to say, the ex's) house.

So you've decided to move out. It may have already happened during the separation period, or it may be many years later. No matter what, when you go you will inevitably find things that are reminiscent of the life you shared with the ex: photos, notes, letters, books inscribed to you both, your wedding book, a tie she gave you.

Forget nostalgia. Put all that stuff in a box and send it to her. Some of this stuff needs to go before the new girl comes into your life.

STUFF TO GIVE TO THE EX – BEFORE YOUR NEXT GIRL COMES ALONG:

- ➤ ANY photograph of you and the ex kissing/hugging – or even standing together – especially any photographs that are framed.
- ➤ Monogrammed towels with her initials (with YOUR last name).
- ➤ The everyday china.
- ➤ ANY amorous note/letter either of you wrote to each other.
- ➤ YOUR WEDDING BOOK.
- ➤ Cutsie cards, stuffed animals – any insider jokes stuff between you and your ex.

Here's why: It is the ultimate gesture of peace and closure. Aside from that, it appeals to your vindictive side -- it gets the monkey off your back and on to hers. Plus, it shows her you are over her.

But most importantly, it'll save you pain later. Let me explain. If the ex doesn't take the whole box and burn it (which she won't), her next boyfriend or husband will inevitably come across parts of it. He'll have to be a pretty secure fellow for it not to get to him. Get where I'm going with this? In a single step you've avoided all that same static from your girlfriend or next wife.

And you've heaped it on the ex.

STUFF THAT'LL BE TOUGHER TO GET RID OF BEFORE THE NEXT GIRL COMES ALONG.
DON'T ASK. JUST DO IT.

- ➢ The Tiffany watch with the loving inscription on the back.
- ➢ Sterling picture frames with your wedding date on them.
- ➢ The racehorse named after the ex.
- ➢ The speedboat named after the ex.

Photoshop her out of any photos you may want to keep around, and get an engraver to eliminate any sign of your previous life from the platinum or silver.

Sell the racehorse cheap, she was a loser anyway.

KIDS 3

Once the divorce is finalized the situation with the children will settle down. Kids are amazingly resilient and adaptive and they will settle into their new life.

Just provide for them as best you can, be their cheerleader, and over time you will be repaid many times over. Sometimes parents try to "brainwash" their kids saying ugly things about the ex. This is the lowest of the low. But the good news is it backfires every time:

> - Kids wonder about the good judgment of the brainwashing spouse. *"If you think he's such a monster, you sure were stupid to marry him."* They may not say this at 7, but they do at 17. Often, if necessary.
> - Kids grow up. They form their own opinions about each of their parents, and if one has been lying to them about the other, they'll sniff that out over time and they'll come to regard the liar as unreliable, petty and maybe even nuts.
> - Criticizing the ex to the kids is always a frustrating experience for the criticizer because kids only have two parents and most kids won't agree that their mom's a tramp or their dad's a monster, or whatever for long. After a while, they won't even go along with it. So if you can't convince the kid, and all you're doing is making the kid uncomfortable – or worse still, defensive of the other parent, what's the point?
> - Sometimes a mother who feels she was wronged by the termination of the marriage wants her kids to find their new life miserable. This gives her a way of blaming dad for the mess he made. But kids are way too self-centered to accommodate these moms for long. Sure, they'll be miserable for a little while, but soon enough, they'll realize they're being made miserable -- by their mom.

Many kids get over their parents' divorce pretty quickly, which is to say their new life becomes their new normal. Their lives are their lives and their divorced parents are just another aspect of life to which they have adapted. Not only that, but by the time they get to high school, many of their friends' parents are divorced too. And some of their friends' parents' divorces and remarriages were, amazing as it may seem to you, spectacularly messier than yours.

FRIENDS

There's a myth that a divorced couple can be friends. It's not so, at least while the children they share are young.

Oftentimes it appears these two are friends because the one who didn't want to break it off is hoping by being sweet, sweet, sweet he or she can bring the other one back. And the one who broke it off is too guilty to say *"Forget it, lose my number."* So they appear to be friends and each one is bending his or her head into a pretzel.

The only sane relationship between divorced couples is a business-like one regarding their jointly held start-up investment: their children.

There are occasional instances in which a couple marries, divorces and then remarries one another. These cases may give hope to some of those pretzel-heads who call themselves "friends." But in general adults, especially straight adult males, do not have friends among the opposite sex who are still in their childbearing years. Something else is going on on one side or the other, it may just not have happened yet.

There is one notable exception to this rule that applies mostly to big personalities with lots of extra money. I have several pals who fall into this category. It can be the case that their wives are glad to be rid of them on a day-to-day basis (and they are, especially if they are the beneficiaries of generous settlements) but that the wives also sincerely enjoy the antics and the glitz and glamour that brought them together in the first place. This is most often so with "public" people, especially performers. On the flip side, the guy with the big personality still enjoys the ex's company – especially if she's still pretty – and so they can countenance one another occasionally.

In the case of two very large personalities who were once married, from time to time they can all get together with their new spouses/girlfriends/boyfriends and the kids for a ski trip together. These get-togethers are often satisfactory for the ex's but the new spouses and the children complain of exhaustion when the trip is over. The stage wasn't big enough to hold the two of them during the marriage, and it hasn't gotten any bigger.

Year in and year out, the best way for ex-spouses to become friends again is to be there for their shared kids – of course, when they're minors, but also when they're starting out life after college, making new families and becoming real adults. Having successful children together, and being there for them, begets a sincere friendship.

Holidays

Scheduling vacations between two households, especially when there are several children involved who attend different schools, requires special talents. Maybe if you work in the State Department and have gained experience in picking through the difficult personalities and challenging logistics of official visits, you can do it with grace. But most of us cannot. Yet we must. Especially in the early years, once you've become accustomed to having your kids around on Christmas morning or at Thanksgiving dinner, it can make you feel pretty lousy to be alone.

Here's how to handle the logistics. Admittedly it's a cop-out, but look for a leader among the children who can work out the details. This won't happen until the first one is old enough to drive a car. The older they get, the more opinions they'll have, and the more the details of the visit will be imposed upon you by them. Your holiday visitation attitude should at that point be: "If it's good with the kids, it's good with me." Try to get this settled with a week or so lead time.

Then:

> Arrange to spend congenially with a girlfriend or family member the part of the holiday the kids will be spending with the ex.
> Lower your expectations of what a perfect Christmas should be.
> This is not a guy thing to do, but think in advance about presents.
> Try to get the ex to tell you more or less what she's giving each child so you don't duplicate or, worse still, compete.
> Some ex's exchange presents. It's one of those pretzel-head things.

➤ Make your own new traditions, and you'll help make the holidays special. This is what holidays are supposed to be. If the new tradition's a hit, the kids will clamor for it next year. If you don't know how to do this kind of thing, and certainly not all dads do, ask a lady you know and trust who gives good parties. She'll have plenty of ideas. Pick the ones you like.

➤ If you stay in the house, don't try to recreate the traditions you had with mom – it's a great reminder of the good old days and the kids will urge you again to try to get back together. (OMG – round two?!)

This is your new life and you'll find yourself enjoying the new traditions soon enough. Be adventuresome. Take lots of pictures. Your kids are growing up fast.

MOVING ON

Like Jack Kerouac, the merry pranksters and many Americans, I love life on the road. The people who are with you in the car are your universe. Everything else is shrinking in importance as it fades away in the rear view mirror. Life on the road is symbolic of two very important concepts now: living in the moment and looking forward.

You've survived a miserable experience and your life is back in your hands. Now you'll be able to look at the other gentlemen you know who are going through a nasty divorce and you can reassure them they'll survive.

A couple of thoughts before you head now into the sunset:
You've taken a huge financial hit. Get with a financial planner or someone who's smart about money, and plan your financial future.

You've taken a huge emotional hit too. Size that up for yourself. Don't ignore it. Here are the remedies in rank order:

1. More sports (playing, not watching)

2. More female companionship. Modern technology has changed the dating scene a thousand-fold for the better since the last time you were single. You need no longer be limited in your choices to the women at the office, at the country club, or those you may randomly meet at a wedding or out to dinner. That was then. Look on this book's website, www.gentlemansguidetodivorce.com , under "Survival Gear" for links to providers of responsible online dating services

3. A shrink

If you're drinking more than you used to (or taking anything else as a way of inducing amnesia) go to Remedy 3.

THE NEXT WIFE

Most importantly, DON'T do anything quickly. Date for a while – even if you don't find it fun. And when you do find someone interesting, hang out for a while. Don't rush into your next contractual relationship, i.e. marriage.

It is very reasonable to ask yourself why you need to marry again. If you want to have more kids, sure. But if not, why? An important note: If you decide not to marry, be sure never to present yourself for convenience as husband and wife. Do not, for example, sign into a hotel or inn as Mr. & Mrs. _____ (your last name here). From where you are today to a "common law marriage" is no great distance. The test is whether you both presented yourselves, even temporarily, as husband and wife. If you did, you can be sued for divorce again. Or, after your death if she decides to press her case, she may be entitled to as much as a third of your statutory estate.

But let's say you decide to marry again just for traditional reasons and to provide a good example for the kids. Great. What's her story?

THE TROPHY WIFE:
Some guys go fishing in the 25-plus-year-younger pond. You'll have a ball while you're dating her, but within a short time, she'll be holding the reins and you'll be wondering what you were thinking. Think about it, unless she is really insecure financially or otherwise, why else would she be fishing in the much-older pond? Sure, you're a catch – but you've got kids, a psycho ex-wife, and the body isn't what it was 25 years ago. And are you ready to see that cute nubile thing grumpy and pregnant with your next round of kids? Remember how in the first round you became far less important to her once the babies joined the party?

A trophy wife is a solid way forward – if you really enjoy the divorce experience.

The way your previous marriage ended may tell you something about whether you are the marrying kind or not. Be honest about this. If you're not, do everyone a favor and stay single. Hey, lots of guys have a ball being the old roue.

Choosing a wife:
If you are the marrying type, make sure
> ➤ she isn't a friend of the ex's.
> ➤ she's easygoing.
> ➤ she comes from approximately your socio-economic background.
> ➤ she shares some of your interests (and isn't *acting* like she does).
> ➤ she won't resent your kids, but might instead become their friend.
> ➤ she wants to build a new life, not inhabit your old one.
> ➤ she loves you – even if you're poor.

No worries, no hurries. She's out there looking for you right now.

Glossary

Affidavit-a sworn statement.

Cohabitation-living together under the same roof with an implication that the parties are engaged in sexual relations.

Condonation-an aggrieved spouse engages in condonation when, after he or she has learned their spouse has engaged in sexual relations outside the marriage, he or she implies their condoning of such behavior by resuming sexual relations as husband and wife.

Confidentiality agreement-A contract in which someone agrees to keep information secret in exchange for compensation.

Custody-The right given by a Court to make decisions on behalf of a minor or incompetent person regarding, but not limited to, their finances, education, and medical care.

Custody Evaluator- a person who may be a psychologist who is appointed by the Court to find facts and make recommendations to the Judge regarding children's issues.

Deposition-the taking and recording of testimony under oath with a court reporter as a part of pre-trial investigation. Questions are permitted by attorneys from both sides.

Guardian ad litem-a person who may be an attorney who is appointed by the Court to take legal action on behalf of a minor or minors. Guardians, like Custody Evaluators, also make recommendations to the judge regarding children's issues.

Inclination and opportunity-a common test for proving adulterous behavior before a court.

Joint custody-a court's determination that both parents shall have a voice in medical, educational, financial and other matters of responsibility for a child.

Mediation-a non-binding and informal attempt to resolve a legal dispute through the active participation of a third party (mediator) who works to find points of agreement and lead those in conflict to a fair resolution of their dispute.

No fault divorce-dissolutions of marriages in which neither spouse is required to show or assume fault or marital misconduct.

Separation agreement-a court-decreed right to live apart with the rights and obligations of divorced persons, but without divorce. For example, child support and alimony may be paid and a division of property may be effectuated and sanctioned by the court. After a set term, typically six months or a year, separation is grounds for divorce.

Temporary Order-The judge's ruling that follows the Temporary Hearing in which he makes child support, alimony, visitation schedule, custody and other determinations as a way of beginning to settle a divorce.

Trophy wife-Don't lose your divorce attorney's number.

Visitation-When a child or children are with one of their parents or guardians.

Visitation schedule-a schedule sanctioned by the Family Court Judge that proscribes when the respective parents or guardians will have the children. This schedule includes not just the school week and weekends, but holidays, vacations and birthdays.

Custody Fight Coming?

E.B. Gunn's companion book to this book, *The Gentleman's Guide to Cooking Through a Child Custody Battle,* is a no-nonsense guidebook to the essentials of life with the kids during a custody fight. The book looks like it might be a cookbook, and it is a book with recipes that kids love.

But *The Gentleman's Guide to Cooking Through a Child Custody Battle* is much more than that.

Techniques for handling the Guardian ad litem? They're here. Trouble with the Custody Evaluator? Here's the trouble-shooting manual. Tricks for cutting the ex off at the pass when she tries to pull a fast one? They're here! Time for a timely counter-punch. Here's how! Want to stay one step ahead of the neighbors, the children's teachers, their coaches and shrinks, all of whom may end up on the witness stand at your next custody hearing? They're here!! Ways of keeping the kids on your team without breathing an ill word about the ex? They're here too!!!

Here's the thing. In a custody fight you have to "Out-Parent" the Ex ... and show it to the Judge. That means cooking the chow yourself at your house and making it fun. It Means Out-Cooking The Ex! It's also patching the kids up when they fall. It's being the judge and jury. It's helping with homework. It's bedtime stories and good-night kisses. And much more.

Here's the Playbook. The first ever written!

You can pay lawyers and shrinks tens of thousands, or you can get it here for less than you'll pay for your next good cigar.

Go to www.gentlemansguidetodivorce.com for more.

Made in the USA
Lexington, KY
13 December 2012